M000198047

Other books in the series:

Prophet Muhammad ﷺ

Abu Bakr as-Siddiq ؓ

Umar ibn al-Khattab ؓ

Uthman ibn Affan ؓ

Hasan and Husayn İbn Ali ؓ

Khadija bint Khuwaylid ؅

Fatima ؅ bint Muhammad ﷺ

Khalid ibn al-Walid ؓ

THE AGE OF BLISS

AISHA
BINT ABU BAKR

ÖMER YILMAZ

NEW JERSEY • LONDON • FRANKFURT • CAIRO • JAKARTA

TUGHRA
BOOKS

New Jersey

Translated by Asiye Gülen
Edited by Clare Duman

Published by Tughra Books
335 Clifton Ave., Clifton,
NJ, 07011, USA

www.tughrabooks.com

Library of Congress Cataloging-in-Publication Data Available

ISBN: 978-1-59784-376-8

Printed in Canada

TABLE OF CONTENTS

The Dream That Came True

*P*rophet Muhammad, peace and blessings be upon him, was dreaming. In his dream, Archangel Gabriel (Jibril) was showing him someone. It was no other than his best friend, Abu Bakr's, may Allah be pleased with him, daughter, Aisha, may Allah be pleased with her. She was wearing clothes as white as milk. "This is your wife," Gabriel said. As he lifted the cover from her head, the noble Prophet saw her face. The dream heralded that this event would soon come to pass.

Two years earlier, the noble Prophet had lost his first wife, Khadija, may Allah be pleased with her. Living alone with his three daughters, he had been lonely and in need of a companion. His relative, Hawla, may Allah be pleased with her, saw his loneliness and asked if he wanted to remarry. The blessed Prophet agreed this would be a good idea but he hadn't decided who he was going to marry. Hawla was ready to help him. In her opinion, the only person worthy of the title of the wife of the noble Prophet was Aisha. After gaining his agreement, Hawla went directly to Abu Bakr's and his wife, Umm Ruman, may Allah be pleased with her, and gave them the news. Abu Bakr and his family were very happy.

Despite his joy at the prospect of the marriage, Abu Bakr had some questions in his mind. He and the blessed Prophet were as close as brothers and he wondered if this closeness would create problems for the marriage. In the age of ignorance, people didn't approve of marrying the daughters of one's close friends. Another problem was that Abu Bakr had already promised Aisha to another family. However, none of these obstacles were insurmountable. The noble Prophet assured Abu Bakr that their friendship would not affect the marriage. The family that had requested Aisha were worried about Abu

Bakr's friendship with the noble Prophet. In those days, being close to the Messenger of Allah meant facing extreme hardship and fighting against the polytheists in Mecca. Abu Bakr realized their worries and asked them if they were still insisting on the marriage. When he heard that they weren't, he returned home content. Now there was nothing left standing in the way of the marriage between Aisha and the blessed Prophet.

Emigration

The blessed Prophet often visited Abu Bakr at home. During these visits he would tell Aisha's mother to be kind and respectful to her. One day, the Messenger of Allah visited Abu Bakr in the noontime. This was unusual; due to the heat people usually slept at this time and the noble Prophet never visited people at this time of the day. However, these days were different. The blessed Prophet was facing enormous opposition from the Meccan polytheists who were conspiring all kinds of evils against him and the Muslims. The Messenger of Allah was intending to inform Abu Bakr about these plans and give him the news that they would emigrate to Medina.

Seeing Abu Bakr's daughters, Asma and Aisha, in the room the noble Prophet told Abu Bakr to ask them to leave. Abu Bakr trusted that his daughters wouldn't breathe a word of what they heard, "May my father be sacrificed for you, O Messenger of Allah. They are your family." Hearing this, the noble Prophet agreed that they could remain with them.

The blessed Prophet gave Abu Bakr the news that Allah had given him permission to emigrate. "Are we going to do this together, O Messenger of Allah," he asked.

"Yes, together," came the reply.

Abu Bakr had been waiting for this news for a long time. He had been hoping that he would accompany the noble Prophet on this journey and had prepared two camels for this purpose. He was so happy hearing the news, tears streamed down his cheeks.

Preparing for the Emigration

Since that day, the only topic discussed in Abu Bakr's house was the emigration. Along with her mother and sister, Aisha started the preparations for the journey. The noble Prophet and Abu Bakr planned to meet late at night and travel to Mount Thawr where they would hide in a cave. Meanwhile, the Messenger of Allah had hidden Ali in his own bed as a decoy to ruin the plans of the polytheists. Abu Bakr's house was under surveillance and he had to escape from a window to meet the blessed Prophet. They headed out to climb Mount Thawr together.

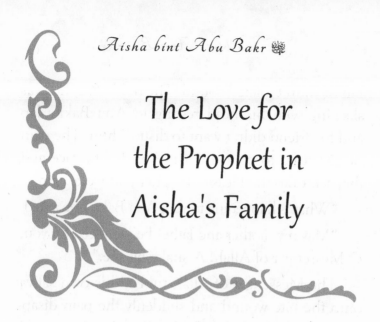

The Love for the Prophet in Aisha's Family

The house where Aisha grew up was full of love for the noble Prophet over anybody else. One of the best examples of this was shown by Abu Bakr, in the Cave of Thawr.

As soon as he entered the cave, Abu Bakr tore up his own clothes to stuff all the holes to prevent snakes and scorpions or other deadly creatures from entering. When he had finished the cloth there was still one hole remaining. He used the heel of his foot to block this hole. A little while later, a snake tried to enter the cave from that hole and, finding it blocked by Abu Bakr's foot, he bit it hard. Feeling a sharp, intense pain, Abu Bakr clenched his teeth

7

but he didn't make a sound. The noble Prophet was sleeping with his head resting in Abu Bakr's lap and his friend didn't want to disturb him. The pain caused tears to course down Abu Bakr's face and they fell onto the blessed Prophet and woke him.

"What is happening to you, Abu Bakr?" he asked.

"May my mother and father be sacrificed for you, O Messenger of Allah! A snake bit me."

The Messenger of Allah rubbed his own saliva onto the bite wound and suddenly the pain disappeared and Abu Bakr's heel returned to its normal shape. It was as if the snake had never bit him.

It wasn't only Abu Bakr who showed such loyalty to the noble Prophet in that cave. As soon as it was apparent who was in the cave, a pigeon flew down to it and protected him from discovery by building her nest in front of the entrance and laying eggs. A spider also protected him by weaving its web over the entrance of the cave to make it appear as if no one had entered.

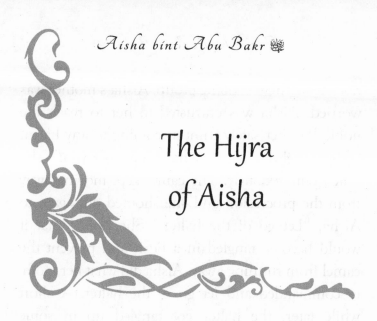

The Hijra of Aisha

onths had passed since the noble Prophet and Abu Bakr's arrival in Medina but Aisha was still waiting in Mecca, desperate for news. One day her patience was rewarded with a visit from her brother, Abdullah, may Allah be pleased with him. Seeing him full of happiness and joy, Aisha knew there had to be some good news. Abu Bakr had written to his son instructing him to bring his mother and sisters to Medina. Now it was time for Aisha to be reunited with her father and the blessed Prophet.

Aisha's journey to Medina was long and tedious. At one point, Aisha's camel started to become separated from the rest of the group. Aisha's mother was worried. Aisha was entrusted to her to reach the noble Prophet safely without coming to any harm. "Oh, daughter, what is happening to you?" she called out anxiously. The camel kept moving away from the procession and she shouted out again to Aisha, "Let go of the halter." She hoped that it would become tangled in a bush and prevent the camel from running away. Aisha did what her mother commanded and let go of the halter. A short while later, the halter got tangled up in some branches and the camel stopped. Aisha's mother was very relieved.

Medina

fter a long and arduous journey, Aisha finally reached Medina. Her months of longing were at an end and with them the troubled days in Mecca came to a close. Despite having much to be thankful for, Aisha was immediately greeted with upsetting news. Her father, unused to the climate in Medina, had caught the plague.

Aisha rushed to her father's side and cried, "Father, how are you feeling?" But the answer wasn't what she wanted to hear.

"Everyone is welcoming a new day in their homes. But death is closer to us than the strings on our feet."

The other sick people lying near Abu Bakr were in no better condition than he was. Seeing their situation, Aisha went immediately to the blessed Prophet and said, "It's as if they have lost their minds because of the fever and disease. They are talking to themselves deliriously."

The state of his closest friend, Abu Bakr, pained the noble Prophet deeply. He raised his holy hands and prayed, "O Allah, make us love Medina just as you made us love Mecca. Make this a healthy place. Make our measurements and scales plentiful and take this disease away from here to Juhfa."

The noble Prophet's prayer was soon answered and Aisha's father and the others were cured of the disease.

The Marriage

O n arrival in Medina, the blessed Prophet stayed as a guest in the house of Abu Ayyub al-Ansari. When Aisha arrived she stayed in her father's house as she and the noble Prophet were not yet married. Soon after, Archangel Gabriel brought the news that their wedding should be solemnized. Eager to marry Aisha but without the necessary dowry, the blessed Prophet looked for an answer to his problem. The solution was to come from no other than his dear friend Abu Bakr, "O Messenger of Allah, is there something preventing us from being under the same roof as your family?" he asked.

"The money for the bride," replied the noble Prophet.

For Abu Bakr, this was no reason to delay such a fortuitous marriage. The blessed Prophet was more important to him than any money could be. He told the blessed Prophet the amount and immediately gave him the money to pay the bride. His generosity didn't end here. He also helped build a room for the noble Prophet next to the mosque.

The blissful house of the Messenger of Allah and Aisha was ready. All that was left to complete were the marriage nuptials and as soon as the month of Shawwal started, the couple married. Marrying in Shawwal corrected a misunderstanding from the Age of Ignorance when people believed that getting married between two festivals was bad luck. The noble Prophet changed this belief by marrying Aisha in Shawwal.

It was time for Aisha to start her new life with the noble Prophet. It was her mother's duty to prepare her for this next stage of her life. One day, at mid-morning, Aisha was with her friends when her mother came and collected her. Not aware of what was happening, Aisha arrived next to the blessed Prophet with her friends, out of breath. The Messenger of Allah offered her a bowl of milk which she shyly refused, unable to look him in the eye. Her friends encouraged her to accept his offer and, taking their advice, Aisha took the bowl from the hands of the noble Prophet and drank. The blessed Prophet told Aisha to offer the milk to her friends, but they also refused, saying they weren't hungry.

"Hunger and lying do not belong together," said the blessed Prophet to them.

Taking their opportunity to speak with the beloved Prophet, Aisha's friends asked him, "O Messenger of Allah, if someone says he is not hungry even though he is, does this count as a lie?"

"Yes, as lies are written as lies, so are little lies written as little lies," came the answer.

So, the bowl of milk became the wedding dinner of the noble Prophet and Aisha. Just as he was always the best example for the Muslims to follow, here he guided us with his modest and simple lifestyle.

The Simple Lifestyle of Aisha

*A*isha led a simple lifestyle starting with her home. Her house was just a few square meters wide, a little room next to the mosque. The walls of the house were plastered with clay, the palm fibers above were the roof, so low that anyone standing up in the room could touch it. A wool covering protected the roof against rain. The entrance was a single wooden door. We can imagine the size of the house from the Aisha's own words, "If the Messenger of Allah was praying while I was sleeping he would touch my feet and I would have to pull them back. Only then could he lie prostrate."

Aisha did not even have an oil lamp to light her house at night. Sometimes, she was only aware that the noble Prophet had left her side when she reached out and felt nothing. She used to say, "There were so many nights when there was no lamp or anything like it glowing in our house. Even if we had lamp oil we would have to use it to cook."

Aisha told her nephew, Urwa, may Allah be pleased with him, about the simple life she led with the blessed Prophet. "We looked at the new moon. After the first, there would be a second and then a third but still there would be no light in our Prophet's home."

"But what did you eat? How did you get by?" Urwa asked.

"Dates and Zamzam water."

During her life with the blessed Prophet, Aisha did not have the chance to eat her fill with bread for more than three days in a row. The day he died, she only had some barley to eat. Even after he passed away, she still did not have enough to eat.

The Messenger of Allah and Aisha did not have to live such a frugal life. This was their choice. One day, a woman was visiting Aisha when she saw the beloved Prophet's bed, which was stuffed with fibers. She sent a bed stuffed with wool as a gift for Aisha. When the blessed Prophet arrived home, he asked, "What is that, Aisha?"

"O Messenger of Allah, a woman came to the house and saw your bed and then gave this as a gift," she answered.

"Send it back. I swear to Allah that if I wanted, He would make the mountains obey me and would turn them into gold and silver."

Aisha bint Abu Bakr

Aisha's Sense of Sharing

*A*isha was a generous person and liked to share whatever she had with people in need. One day, a poor person came to Aisha and she gave them whatever she could as charity. Later, she wanted to call that person again. When the noble Prophet heard, he interrupted and said, "Do not follow the things that you give so that the same doesn't happen to you."

One day, the blessed Prophet noticed that Aisha was wearing silver rings on her hand. "What are those Aisha?" he asked.

"I am wearing these to look beautiful for you, O Messenger of Allah," she said.

"Did you pay the *zakah* for those?"

"No"

"They will lead you to Hell," he told her.

After this warning, Aisha gave whatever she possessed to the poor, keeping nothing for herself.

Encouraging her good behavior, the noble Prophet said, "If you want to reunite with me (in the afterlife) you must pass through this world like a traveler. Do not get involved with the (ungenerous) rich. Do not change your clothes until you cannot use them anymore."

The Messenger of Allah advised all his family, including Aisha, "If mankind has two valleys full of wealth, he would want the third. Nothing but the soil satisfies man. However, wealth is given to make the Daily Prayers possible and to enable us to pay *zakah*. There is no doubt that those who repent are forgiven by Allah."

Aisha and her Interest in Children

*A*isha used to keep toys for the children to play with when they came to her house. One day, the blessed Prophet saw her with a winged horse and asked, "What is that, Aisha?"

"A horse!"

"Does a horse have wings?"

Aisha showed her knowledge of the Qur'an with her answer, "Didn't Solomon's horse have wings?"

Her witty answer amused the noble Prophet, making him laugh.

Aisha's Love for the Prophet

isha loved the noble Prophet dearly and would not exchange the times she shared with him for anything else. Sometimes, the beloved Prophet would sleep with his head lying in Aisha's lap. She would be so careful not to disturb him, even if she was in pain or discomfort.

One day, the blessed Prophet said, "Aisha! Look, this is Gabriel! He sends his greetings."

"May Allah's blessings, mercy and grace be upon him," she responded. "You see what we cannot."

Aisha's words showed her admiration of the noble Prophet's ability to see the Angel of Revelation, Gabriel, when no one else could.

The Prophet's Love for Aisha

The blessed Prophet loved Aisha as much as she loved him. His Companions referred to her as, "Our Prophet's beloved." When they wanted to give him presents, they waited until he was with Aisha because then he was so happy it was as if he was floating on air. Aisha, too, was aware of his love.

When the blessed Prophet was asked whom he loved the most, he answered, "Aisha." When he was asked which man he loved the most he answered, "Her father."

One day, the noble Prophet was invited by a neighbor to have some soup. He asked, "Are you inviting Aisha as well?"

"No," the man replied.

The Messenger of Allah declined the invitation. Some time later, the neighbor came and repeated his invitation. The blessed Prophet asked again, "Are you inviting Aisha as well?"

"Yes," the man answered.

This time, the noble Prophet accepted the invitation.

The reason the blessed Prophet cared about Aisha so much was not just because of his love. One day, he was asked the reason of his love for her and he said that Aisha was the only one from his family who was with him when he received a revelation.

According to the beloved Prophet, Aisha was superior to other women just as *tirit* is superior to other meals. *Tirit* was one of the favorite meals at the time of the noble Prophet.

Entertainment

One festival day, a large group of people had gathered to be entertained by a group with swords and shields. Aisha was at the back, unable to see what was happening. She told the noble Prophet that she wanted to see. "Do you really want that?" he asked.

"Yes," she nodded.

The Messenger of Allah lifted her onto his back so that her cheek was touching his face. Aisha watched the game for a while after which the blessed Prophet asked, "Is that enough now?" He was tired.

"Yes," Aisha replied.

"So go now," he told her.

Race

One day, the noble Prophet was setting out with his army on a campaign. Aisha was with him. Suddenly, the blessed Prophet instructed, "You go ahead," to the army.

Staying behind with Aisha, the Messenger of Allah said to her, "Come on, let's have a race!" The two of them raced against each other and Aisha outran the noble Prophet.

Some time later, Aisha was on another journey with the blessed Prophet. He turned to the people with them and said, "You go ahead." Then, turning to Aisha he said, "Come on, let's have a race!"

Aisha happily accepted the invitation. To do otherwise was unimaginable. This time, the Messenger of Allah won the race. He turned to Aisha smiling and said, "This is the reciprocation of our first race."

Sensitivity Education

*P*art of the Prophetic mission was to teach social ethics to the people and Aisha also learned this from him. Once, Aisha made a barley bun for the noble Prophet. However, as the Messenger of Allah preferred to sleep for a while as soon as he came home, the neighbor's sheep managed to steal the bun and run away. Anxious, Aisha ran after the sheep. The blessed Prophet woke up and called out, "If you catch up, just take the bun. Don't blame your neighbor because of what the sheep did."

The Extent
of Helping

In the time of the noble Prophet, people used to eat the meat of an animal called the star lizard. The blessed Prophet did not like the meat of this animal and he did not eat it. One day, someone brought some of that meat to the noble Prophet's house. As usual, he did not eat the meat. Then, Aisha asked him, "Should I give it to someone in need?"

Aisha's intention was sincere because eating the meat of the star lizard was not forbidden and, if they were not to use it, it was better to give it to someone in need. However, the noble Prophet did not approve of giving something away that he did not eat himself. He turned to Aisha and said, "No, do not give what you do not eat to others."

Aisha's Prayer

Throughout their nine years together, Aisha always took the noble Prophet as her example and because of this, her Prayers were similar to his. The Messenger of Allah spent so much time performing the Night Prayer his feet used to swell. When she described his Prayers, Aisha said, "I cannot even begin to describe the beauty and the length of his Night Prayer."

After performing the Night Prayer, the noble Prophet would sleep then he would wake again to perform the *Tahajjud* Prayer at midnight. A while afterwards, he would wake Aisha to perform her *Witr* and *Tahajjud* Prayers. At the time for the

Morning Prayer, the blessed Prophet would perform the *Sunnah* Prayer and then he would lie down on his right cheek or talk with Aisha. When he was leading the Morning Prayer in the mosque, Aisha would join him from their room and perform the Prayer behind him in the congregation.

Aisha cared about the Night Prayer very much. She said, "Do not neglect getting up at night and performing your Prayer because the Messenger of Allah never abandoned his Night Prayers. If he was sick or tired he performed it sitting down but he never neglected it."

Aisha's Fasting

isha fasted almost every day. She did not stop fasting, even when she was travelling. She also completed her obligations of worship no matter what.

One very hot day, the eve of a holy day, Aisha was fasting and her brother came to visit her. Seeing her sweating heavily he said, "Break your fast."

"I cannot break my fast, because I heard the Messenger of Allah say, 'Fasting on the eve of a holy day is penance for the sins of the previous year.'

Aisha
and Hajj

ne year, Aisha had the chance to perform Hajj, the major pilgrimage, with the noble Prophet. This was the first and last Hajj that the Messenger of Allah performed; his farewell pilgrimage. After he passed away, Aisha was able to perform Hajj several more times.

Her eagerness to perform Hajj was due to a conversation she had with the blessed Prophet. One day, she asked him, "O Messenger of Allah! Why can't we (women) fight in the wars like men?"

Aisha's wishes were sincere. She wanted to find more ways to serve Islam, however, the rules of creation dictated that women were not expected to fight in the same way as men.

The noble Prophet advised her, "The most beautiful and best striving for women is an accepted pilgrimage." This was enough for Aisha. After she received this wisdom she made every effort to perform the pilgrimage and gave the same advice to the people she saw there.

In the early years of the Hajj, the Ka'ba was not very crowded and Aisha was able to circumambulate with everyone else. However, in later years it became very crowded and, not wanting to mix closely with men during the circumambulation, Aisha waited until it was quieter or completed her circumambulation in a wide circle.

Aisha and

Sadaqa

*A*isha set an example for all Muslims by giving *sadaqa* (charity) and helping the poor. She shared whatever she possessed with people in need, even giving away presents she had been given.

When he was caliph, Muawiya sent her dresses, silver and other valuables to use. As soon as she saw them she started to cry, "Our dear Prophet could not find any of these."

She divided them and sent them to people in need and, by the end of the day, nothing was left of them.

One day, Aisha was given baskets full of grapes. She immediately gave them out to the poor. However, she did not notice that someone spared some for her own house. When she saw them, she was surprised. "What is that?" she asked.

She understood that the grapes had been spared for her, but she was upset that they were not distributed to the poor with the others. "Just one branch, is it? I swear to Allah that I will not touch or eat it," she said.

One day, someone went to Aisha and asked her for food. Aisha gave him a sack with bread in it. After this, another person came. This person was not of sound mind. Aisha called him over and fed him the food from her own hands. He ate his fill and left. When people asked her about her behavior, she responded, "The Messenger of Allah said, 'Treat people according to their circumstances.' How could I act in any other way when I know that?"

When Umar was caliph, he sent Aisha a sack of gold. This pulled at her heartstrings. Not able to hold back her tears, Aisha distributed all the gold, but that was not enough for her. She begged Allah that she would never again be given such a gift. She had spent years with the noble Prophet, the beloved of Allah, and had learned from him how to live as a normal person among the people. Her whole life was spent in this way.

One person who visited her related their experience. "I visited Aisha after the Messenger of Allah passed away. She was crying and she offered me some food. Then she said, 'I want to cry until my eyes are dried out. I do not want to put a bite of food in my mouth.' I was surprised. 'Why?' I asked. 'The Messenger of Allah said, 'Treat people according to their situations.' How can I act differently when I know that?"

One day, a woman with two daughters in her arms, visited Aisha. Aisha offered her three dates. Taking the dates, the woman gave one each to her daughters, then split the third between them, saving nothing for herself. Aisha related this to the noble Prophet.

"For what she did, Allah will give her a place in Paradise and redeem her from Hell," he prophesied.

One day, a needy person visited Aisha. Aisha looked around her and found some bread to give the woman. Aisha was fasting that day and had intended to use that bread to break her fast. Someone noticed and warned her, "There is nothing left to break your fast."

Unperturbed, Aisha instructed, "Give it to her," and the bread was given to the woman. Towards evening Aisha was given some presents that included some mutton and bread. When it was time to break the fast, Aisha called out to the person who had warned her not to give away her bread, "Here, take this," she said jokingly, "after all, it's better than your dry bread!"

Aisha learned how to share what she had with Allah's creation from the blessed Prophet. She had heard him say, "Even if it is half a date (give it to the poor), save yourself from the Hellfire." She never stopped acting upon this advice.

One day, when they sacrificed an animal for the sake of Allah, Aisha gave away most of the meat to the poor. All that was left was the shoulder bone. Returning home, the noble Prophet asked, "What happened to the sacrifice? What is left?"

"I gave it all away," Aisha replied. "We only have the shoulder bone."

The blessed Prophet was pleased with her. This was what he wished for, because Allah had promised that whatever was given in His Name would be appreciated. When something was given for the sake of Allah alone, the good deed would be written irascibly and that which was given would gain perpetuity. Allah gives to those who have given for Allah.

Aisha and Covering the Body

*a*isha was very careful to make sure she covered her body and covered even before people who couldn't see her. One day, a blind man was visiting her and she hid behind a curtain. Surprised, the man asked, "Are you hiding from me? I can't even see you."

"You may not see me, but I see you," Aisha replied.

Aisha taught her close students whatever she knew by practicing it herself. One of them had a slave named Salim. One day, Salim asked Aisha to teach him how to perform ablution. Salim was considered as kin because he belonged to someone close, so

Aisha was free to mix with him. A while after, Salim approached Aisha again and said, "O Mother of the Believers, pray for me!"

"Why?" asked Aisha.

"Allah saved me from slavery," replied Salim.

"Very well," said Aisha and closed the curtain because now that Salim did not belong to someone close to her, she could no longer mix with him.

The Extraordinary Events That Aisha Witnessed

The Trench War lasted for nearly a month. The enemies had finally left the trench, which had been dug around Medina and the noble Prophet had returned to the city with his Companions. Putting down their weapons, they were taking a rest. The Messenger of Allah was at home with Aisha when she noticed a movement in front of the door. Looking through the opening, she saw an enormous man dressed in armor and a turban, mounted on horseback. Shaking the dust of him he was calling to the blessed Prophet. As soon as he heard the voice, the Messenger of Allah jumped up and ran to the door. It was none other than the Arch-angel Gabriel.

He spoke to the noble Prophet, "O Messenger of Allah. You are very quick to drop your weapons. We angels never put down our weapons since the enemy arrived. And now, we are returning having followed them to make sure they couldn't counterat-tack. Allah made them suffer a major defeat. May Allah forgive you. Why did you step aside when we were still at it? Come on! We are going because Allah commanded you to fight the Quraysh tribe. Now I am going to their land to shake their castle with the angels. Gather your Companions and come."

This invitation astonished Aisha.

The Messenger of Allah entreated, "My Com-panions are very tired. Can they not have a few days rest?"

Gabriel insisted, "Do not wait! Jump down their throats. I swear to Allah I am going to crush them like a sledgehammer and tear down them and their country."

Then, Gabriel turned and started to move with the others behind him. Aisha had followed the conversation carefully. When the blessed Prophet returned, she asked him, "O Messenger of Allah, who were you talking to?"

"Did you see him?" asked the noble Prophet.

"Yes, I did," said Aisha.

"Who did it look like?"

"Your friend, Dihya."

"That was Gabriel," said the blessed Prophet. "He commanded me to advance on the Quraysh tribe."

Tayammum

The war was over and the noble Prophet was returning to Medina with his Companions. They took a break at a place called, Zatu'l-Jaysh. While they were resting, Aisha noticed that a necklace her elder sister, Asma, had given her was missing. She had entrusted it to her so she had to find it at all cost. Aisha searched around in the dark but could not find the necklace. Eventually, she told the blessed Prophet who got up and started searching too. Those who noticed them, also searched but no one could find the necklace. Giving up, they decided to rest. The Messenger of Allah rested his head on Aisha's lap. Meanwhile, some of the people were getting bored looking for the necklace and the army had run out of water. They mentioned it to Abu Bakr. It would soon be time for the Morning Prayer but there was no water to perform the ablution. Abu Bakr became angry and approached Aisha, saying, "You detained all those people and our Prophet here. Nobody has any water."

Aisha was in a difficult position. The Messenger of Allah was asleep on her lap and she didn't want to disturb him. Then, the noble Prophet awoke. It was time for the Morning Prayer, but there was not enough water for the ablution. Everyone was murmuring discontentedly until they noticed something different about the blessed Prophet. The doors of heaven had opened and a revelation was being sent to the beloved Prophet.

When the Messenger of Allah received a revelation, he would start pouring sweat, even in winter. When the revelation ended, the noble Prophet informed his Companions about it. According to this revelation, when there is no water available, they could cleanse themselves with clean soil.

Everyone became happy and was smiling. Even Abu Bakr, who a moment earlier had been so angry with his daughter, was now saying, "What a blessed person you are! Look, because of the delay that you caused, Allah bestowed blessing and easiness on people."

They performed the Morning Prayer and continued their journey. When a camel stood up, Aisha noticed a glittering necklace that had been underneath it. Looking closely she was sure it was the necklace her sister had given her to look after. Aisha was doubly happy after this.

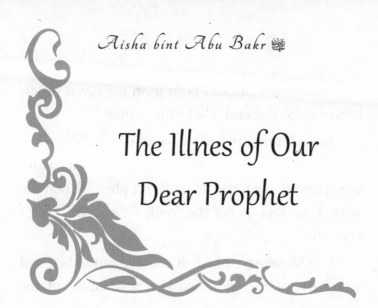

The Illnes of Our Dear Prophet

The noble Prophet had been to the graveyard to attend the funeral of one of his friends. On his return home his head started aching and he began to become feverish. Aisha too had a headache. The two of them turned to each other saying, "Oh my head!" Despite his poor condition, which wasn't improving, the noble Prophet still led the Prayers for the congregation in the mosque.

The Messenger of Allah requested from his family to stay with Aisha during his illness. His condition worsened and his fever became so severe it caused him to faint. Regaining consciousness after a short time, he turned to Aisha and said, "Gather water from different wells and pour it on me seven times. I want to go out and talk to the people."

Aisha immediately set about the task. Water was brought from the seven different wells of Medina and was poured over the blessed Prophet. When he started to feel better he said, "Enough! That's enough."

The Messenger of Allah climbed out of bed and stood up, then, with help he was taken to the mosque.

Inside the mosque, he called out to his Companions, "O you people! Come closer. Do not ever turn my grave into an icon that you worship. For those that I have hurt here, come with a stick, hit me and get your due. To those who I have said hurtful things or broken their hearts, come to me, say what is on your mind and get your due."

Someone stood up and said the noble Prophet owed him three dirhams. The beloved Prophet turned to his nephew and told him, "Fadl, give it to him."

Then, the Messenger of Allah started talking about the Medinan Helpers.

"I bequeath to you to appreciate the Helpers because they are very important to me. They performed their part thoroughly and they will be rewarded. But today, the Helpers have become a minority due to the increase in the number of Muslims. Do not forget that they are the cherry on the cake. If you become a manager of them, appreciate what they do right and forgive what they do wrong. Allah set before His servant the beauties of the world and the afterlife. His servant chose the afterlife."

As soon as the noble Prophet finished speaking, a voice was heard from the corner of the mosque, "May my mother and father be sacrificed for you, O Messenger of Allah!"

It was none other than Aisha's father, Abu Bakr. He was a man with strong intuition and heightened perception and he understood that this was a farewell speech.

The Path to Eternity in the Bosom of Aisha

he blessed Prophet's condition was worsening day by day. One day, he asked Aisha, "Did they perform their Prayer yet?"

"No, O Messenger of Allah," she replied. "They are waiting for you."

"Prepare the water so I can perform my ablution."

The Messenger of Allah performed his ablution with the water they prepared. Just as he was leaving for the mosque, he fainted again. When he regained consciousness he asked immediately, "Did they perform their Prayer?"

"No, O Messenger of Allah!" replied Aisha. "They are waiting for you."

The noble Prophet said, "Tell Abu Bakr to lead the Prayer."

Aisha objected, saying, "O Messenger of Allah! Abu Bakr is such a softhearted man; he bursts into tears when he starts reading the Qur'an. Maybe you should choose someone else."

Aisha was probably worried that whoever took the place of the noble Prophet in the *mihrab* would face a lot of criticism and she wanted to save her father from that. But, the blessed Prophet was determined.

"Tell Abu Bakr to lead the Prayer."

Aisha was just as determined as the beloved Prophet. Again she insisted. She did not want it to be her father taking the noble Prophet's place.

The Messenger of Allah spoke decisively, "You are behaving like one of the women who fell out with each other over Joseph. Tell Abu Bakr to be the congregation leader and to lead the Prayer."

When the blessed Prophet was feeling a little stronger, two men helped him to the mosque. Abu Bakr was leading the Noon Prayer. When he saw the noble Prophet arrive, he wanted to step down but the Messenger of Allah motioned for him to continue, he turned to the others and said, "Sit me next to him."

As the days passed, the noble Prophet's illness grew worse. He set his slaves free and gave them six or seven dinars as *sadaqa*. It was as if he was going to give everything away. He divided his weapons between the believers and handed out whatever he had remaining on earth. He planned to leave the earth in the same way he had arrived. There was nothing left to eat in his house so the blessed Prophet's armor was given to a Jewish neighbor in exchange for thirty weight of barley.

Bilal recited the morning call to Prayer. The Companions were performing the Prayer behind Abu Bakr. The Messenger of Allah parted the curtain that separated him from the mosque and saw his Companions for one last time before he departed this life. A sweet smile appeared on his face as he witnessed his community fulfilling their duties towards Allah.

Sensing the presence of the beloved Prophet, Abu Bakr wanted to move aside for the noble Prophet to lead the Prayer. The Messenger of Allah motioned to him to continue and said, "Stay there and finish your Prayer."

Then, he closed the curtain and went to Aisha's room. "What did you do with that gold, Aisha?" he asked.

Aisha went and fetched the gold the noble Prophet was asking about. He took it and started counting, "...five, six, seven."

He said, "How can Muhammad appear before Allah while he has these? Take them and give them away."

The beloved Prophet was nearing the end. He rested his head on Aisha's chest, his dark eyes looking up. Aisha's brother, Abdurrahman entered the room holding a *siwak* (a special stick or root from *arak* tree that is used to cleanse the teeth) in his hand. The Messenger of Allah was looking at it.

"Do you want that?" Aisha asked.

He nodded. Aisha took it from her brother and wanted to give it to the noble Prophet but it was very hard. "Do you want me to wet it for you?" She asked. The blessed Prophet nodded so she softened it and gave it to him. He used it to brush his teeth meticulously.

The last Prophet was about to draw his last breath. Aisha, leaned towards him and heard him murmuring a prayer, "Forgive me and wrap me in Your mercy with the Prophets, martyrs and the righteous ones whom You bestowed Your blessings upon. Accept me into Your Almighty companionship. My Allah! I want Your Almighty companionship. My Allah! I want Your Almighty companionship. My Allah! I want Your Almighty companionship."

The sound of the noble Prophet's prayer tore Aisha's heart out. "He is not going to be with us anymore..."

Aisha found solace in prayer. She took the blessed Prophet's hand into hers and prayed. At that moment, something unexpected happened. The noble Prophet's hand slid from hers to the bowl of water. Aisha felt a piece of her heart break because in that moment, the Messenger of Allah had returned to his exalted Creator.

Aisha wanted to lose herself in her grief. But, as the mother of the believers, the dear Prophet's wife, she needed to be there for the people. She did what was necessary, putting a pillow under the beloved Prophet's head and calling out to the people to deliver the devastating news.

Aisha and Knowledge

Having been with the noble Prophet from a young age, Aisha had gained a lot of knowledge and had improved herself in religious matters. Her intelligence, ability and curiosity about religious matters made her one of the foremost Companions. She questioned the blessed Prophet about everything that came into her mind and lots of things were clarified with her questions. After the Messenger of Allah passed away, her house became a home of wisdom where everyone, young and old, men and women, would come to ask religious questions.

One day, Aisha was asked about the noble Prophet morals. "Didn't you ever read the Qur'an?"

she asked the questioner. "The Messenger of Allah was like the Qur'an."

Another time, she was asked, "Could you tell us about our Prophet's Night Prayers."

Aisha responded to that question with another question again, "Don't your read Surah al-Muzzammil?"

Aisha's Death

*a*isha lived a long life after the noble Prophet passed away. She ensured that the supreme religion of Islam was transmitted properly. During one Ramadan, as she was fulfilling her sacred duty, she was reunited with Allah. Her Funeral Prayer was read by Abu Hurayra, may Allah be pleased with him, a dear friend of the blessed Prophet. A huge crowd attended her funeral. Anyone who heard the news of her death came running to pay their respects to her as she was the beloved wife of the Messenger of Allah and the mother of all the believers.

May Allah bless her and give her soul rest, and make us one of those who are honored with her intercession. (Amin).